As I Breathe

As I Breathe

Dreaming Out Loud

Brandi Tucker

AS I BREATHE
Dreaming out loud

Copyright © Brandi Tucker, 2024

Published by Brandi Tucker, Edmonton, Canada

ISBN:
> 978-1-77354-583-7   Paperback
> 978-1-77354-584-4   ebook

Publication assistance by

PAGEMASTER
PUBLISHING
PageMaster.ca

For my mom and dad. For always being there.

FOREWORD

Brandi, born in 1978, was the second of two children in our family. Even from a young age, she left a lasting impression on everyone she met. When she was eight years old and we lived in Tumbler Ridge, British Columbia, she fell seriously ill with pneumonia in the fall of 1986. Hospitalized at the Chetwynd Hospital for over a week, she faced another challenge on her way home when our pickup truck collided head-on with a large wood truck, causing it to veer off the highway. Brandi hit her head on the dashboard and lost consciousness immediately. Rushed to a specialized children's hospital in Vancouver the next morning, she emerged from a coma after more than a month, her first words being, "I love you, daddy." Despite some permanent damage, she has lived a relatively normal life. At 45 years old, she remains her 'daddy's little girl,' and a beautiful woman with many God-given talents, poetry being her foremost.

This book owes its existence to the persistent efforts of my friend and barber of over 35 years, Shawn Henstridge. For months, he insisted that Brandi's writings should be put into print, and he made it happen. Although every word in the following pages belongs to Brandi, I want to thank you, her mom thanks you, and, certainly Brandi thanks you, for all you've done. You will always be her best 'bud.'

Pete Tucker

Introduction

If there is one thing I hate, it would have to be living with a brain injury. People don't treat you like a person. No, they make it worse by treating you like a victim. I was brain injured when I was eight years old, and I still have a lot of difficulty, even now.

People don't want to get to know me. It seems like everybody has a place to go. But here I am, stuck with questions I may never know the answers to. Like why? Why did this happen to me? Am I being punished by something that is not my fault?

I could have died, but hey, at least I'm living. God and his angels held my chin high. I could have died.

I could read a lost soul to sleep with what I write. Every line is another emotion. I could make an old man cry with my vocabulary and words. I may not look very intelligent or smart, but if you take the time to read what I write you will think differently of me, of yourself, of others, and of the world.

Brandi Tucker

Wild Horses

Wild horses
On the desert wind
Dying from hunger
Of a new beginning
Never can see
What's been fallen
At their feet
Too blind
From the sorrows
Of whatever
Could've been
Constantly wonder
When will they be
Rescued by the
Arms of love?
Saddened streaks
They brush their
Hair back
Each feeling
The same
Yet all feeling
Alone

Missing The Night

Missing the night
In the morning
Wonder where it went
Will we ever have the chance
To again, reflect our lives
On yesterday
The shadows
We carry in our hearts
Are so big
When we dream
Our hearts are bigger
Then we believe life could be
So once again
We are
Missing the night
In the morning

If Every Word I say

If every word I say
Can make you laugh
I'll talk forever
If every song I sing
Can make you dream
You'd dream forever
I love who you are
And where you're from
And what you are made off
I thank God
For giving me
Your hand to hold
And baby
That fragile hand
I hold forever
So, if every word
I say can make you laugh
I will talk forever

I Am A Day Dreamer

I am a day dreamer
Even at night
I lay awake
Pretending someone is holding me
I guess it helps to
Save me from going crazy
From reality
I dream about
Someone actually
Talking to me
Holding me
Being with me
It may be only dreaming
But the ability to dream
Is mine
I am grateful
It is mine
I believe that
If I dream of someone
That person is having
The same dream
About me
I am a day dreamer

The World Will Not Stop Turning

The world will not
Stop turning
Because you are alone
People care
For people like you
Though beautiful people
Care for nothing
You close your eyes
And you see
What you know
In your heart
Is not real
Maybe the world has changed
Maybe you have changed
Praying for the past
You want to
Go back to the future
Wishing someone
Could read your mind
Someone might be
Thinking the same
So, friend
The world will not stop turning
Because you are alone

Anything For You

I'd do anything
For you
But give you up
You hurt me
Through and through
But you know
I am strong
I am strong enough
To say I tried
But far too weak
To say goodbye
No
You'll never
Hear me crying
But you know
Inside
I feel
Like dying
Still, I'd do
Anything for you

Hope Floats

Hope floats
As rivers run
Under the sea
Over the ocean
Kissing the rain
Cards and phone calls
And photographs
Pictures of you
A constant reminder
Of all the things
You get use to
Is there a chance
Here in heaven?
Is there still
Something here to belong
Or do you just
Pick up the pieces
After they fall?

If You Could Have Read My Mind

If you could have
Read my mind
Yesterday
You would not
Be in trouble
Right now
Imagination
Travels
Like a river
Roughly swimming
Across the sea
My mind
Would have told you
Stories
That endlessly
Influence the heart
And the soul
Of someone
In trouble
You would not be in trouble
Right now,
If you could
Have read my mind
yesterday

How's My Girl

How's my girl
She asked
With fear
In her eyes
Didn't need to
Say a thing
A mother can
Always tell
When something
Is not right
I'm scared, mom
She spoke
With a chest ironed grin
Her mother
Looked her daughter in the eye
And realized
She was stronger
Then she gave
Herself credit for
A prayer
Went from
One's eye
To the other
Person's eye
Knowing
That everything
Will be alright

I Love You Still

'Cause in you
I've confidence
So you can
Be untied
For once
Wake up
Who cares about
Those who only
Talk too much
I've seen it all
Go down
Love once made
Your world go 'round
So come on, baby
Come on over
Let me be the one to show you
I'm the one
Who wants to
Hold you tight
You know that
I want to
Every night
'Cause you know
I love you
And I always will
I loved you
Before, babe
I love you still

Over My Head

Holy Moses
Boy, it
Could've been me
Caught up
In the place
I didn't
Want to be
But I'm not
A fool
No
I was
One step ahead
I had to
Let go
Because I
Was over
My head

ALL I CARE ABOUT

Blonde hair
Beautiful eyes
Rosey red lips
Soft enough to kiss
All I care about
Is everything
About you
I can't keep myself
Controlled
When you look
Into my eyes

I Loved You I Lost You

I loved you
I lost you
I found you again
I've been trying
To get down
To the heart of the matter
But my will gets weak
And the memories are scattered
When I'm thinking about
Forgiveness
Yes, maybe forgiveness
Is there a chance for us?
Maybe I'd hold your hand again
Maybe you'd kiss my lips again
I feel secure
In your soft arms
I'm not sure what to say
What to do
What to feel
There's a hole in my heart
That can only be filled by you
And this hole in my heart
Can't be filled
By the things I do
When prayer's role
And wishes would disappear
Please
Oh, please remember
I loved you
I lost you
And I found you again
Thank God, I found you again

BRANDI TUCKER

No More Sadness

No more sadness
Oh yeah
Gonna make you happy
In these days
Of conscience living
We've got to take it slow
Life will pass you by
If you don't slow down
When you smile at me
I can see
A true world of gold
Whenever your hope is gone
I'll give you
The strength you need
To carry on

Friends Forever

We're gonna be friends forever
We're gonna cross that river
We're gonna be together now
We're gonna help each other
And be able to fight for each other
We're gonna be together now
Come on buddy
Shake my hand now
Don't be afraid to make a friend
You know how much I care about you
We'll be best buddies
Until the end
The end of time
Can you see me
Walking down the street
You surely have a picture
To my empty mind

And now I find
I'm walking in
A slow and endless march
And I'm looking for the bright spot
In the sky
But I know
And you know
Our wild dreams
We'll never follow
Heaven or hell
As long as we're together
We'll say amen
I have a wonderful friend
You hear me loud and clear
It's true
I have a lovingly friend
And that friend
Is you

Can't Live Without You

Here he comes
Ooh, he's like an angel
Holds my heart in the palm of his hands
There he lays down
With that old burning desire, baby
I have lived on the outside of everything
Been alone in the dark, oh oh oh
Nothing I can do now
But rap up my lonely heart, baby
I can't live without your
Love and affection
I can't face another night on my own
I'd give up my pride
To save me from being alone
I can't live without your love
Your love
There he goes
Ooh, running away now
Wonder if he'll ever come back again
Deep in my heart

I know that I'm more than a friend, baby
I have lived on the outsides of everything
Been alone in the dark, oh oh oh
Nothing I can do now
But rap up my lonely heart, baby
I can't live without your
Love and affection
I can't face another night on my own
I'd give up my pride
To save me from being alone
I can't live without your love
Your love
You got to have love, love
You got to have faith, faith
You got to have love, love
Now hear my voice
You got to have faith, faith
You got to have love, love
You got to have it all, all
Now make your choice
Will it be love
Or nothing?

I Don't Have Time

I don't have time
To laugh
I don't have time
To cry
All I do is
Everything
This
That
Big things
Small things
I'm a little
Unstable
Too afraid
To look
In the mirror
Afraid that
My future
Will not
Be as good
As my past

Broken Heart

He called her
Long after he broke
Her heart
Was he bothered
By old memories
Has being lonely
Got the best of him
With a fake
Cheerful voice
She talks away
Asking how he's been
Looks in the mirror
She's still crying
Over him
She must
Care a lot more
Then she thought
She ever could
Says she must go now
He says he might call again
She can't believe
He called
Long after he broke
Her broken
Heart

Love Is Not Like This

Love is not
Like this
Love is not
Like no, no, no
Love is not
Like this
On the radio
I thought that
Music mattered
Listen to the news
Hear the songs
Songs that remind you
Of the good times
Songs that remind you
Of the better times
Yet to come
I remember this song
We sang with it
With the windows down
Remember?
I thought
You were nuts
You thought
I was crazy
Love is not
Like this
Love is not like
No, no, no
Love is not
Like this
On the radio

No Time Wasted

Looking back
To the road
I've walked on
I've seen times
An old man
Could only
Dream of
I don't want to
Wait for my life
To be over
I would rather
Know now
What I'm
Doing right
What I'm doing wrong
If I must
Make a few changes
Or improve
A thing
Or two
So be it
I just don't
Have time
To waste time

Eyeing A Stranger

He is different
She thought
Looking across the room
Eyeing a stranger
He must have
A deep soul
The kind that
No one can see
But a blind soul
Can feel
She gently staired
Made a wish
Sent it to heaven
Looked into his eyes
And saw a tear
A tear of sadness?
A tear of joy?
She was unsure
She gently looked away
Feeling as though
Her soul had been
Passed to him
And never again
Returned

THUNDER

Thunder
So loud
So peaceful
You feel
Another moonlight
Coming on
You feel cold
All over
Your cold frozen body
But you find
Thunder exciting
You no longer
Mind being alone
The sound of thunder
Makes your
Soul scream
After the storm
Soft rain runs down
The window
You fall asleep
Knowing that
Everything will
Be alright

As Her Angel

Don't be afraid
She whispers
As he slowly
Dies away
She kisses
His forehead
And wipes her
Tears on
His bare chest
Knowing this would happen
For the longest time
Practiced being brave
Forgot all about that
As his last breath
Whispered
I love you
I only wish
You knew
I love you
She cried
As he died away
Held his heart
Forever
Knowing
He'd come back
To her, someday
As her angel

It's An Addiction

Heads I win
Tails you lose
Ace of hearts
Impossible to find
Love is a gamble
You bet more
Then you ever have
Inside
You know
You shouldn't
But your mind
Has taken control
Of your soul
So, you say
Another hand, Joe
One more hand
Promise yourself
This is your last hand
But it is never
Your last hand
You play
Until you lose
You lose your mind
You lose your soul
To the game
They say it's a game
But no
It's an addition

TIME PASSES BY

Time passes by
As raging rivers flow
Across the ocean
Wild people care
Only for the impossible
Time lasts forever
In their eyes
Wild people
Are all around
But you never
Know who is one
You could be
I could be
Time passes by
As raging rivers flow
Across the ocean
Wild people care
Only for the impossible

Body Language

A bed of roses
He lays her on
They talk for hours
He holds her hand
Kisses her soft
Rosey lips
Tells her everything
He loves about her
Her eyes
Lips
Body
Mind
Heart
Soul
Imagination
He loves her so much
He tries so hard
Not to talk
Too much
But when he does
She gently touches
His lips
And whispers
Hush
And they give
Each other
Body language

Love Into Words

You can't put love
Into words
A touch
Can say a lot
A kiss
Can confuse
The mood
Looking at
Someone
Can express
How you feel
How you make
Someone feel
You can't put love
Into words

I Let You Down

I let you down
You will never know
How sorry I am
But I will
Make it up
To you
If I must
Walk on water
I will
If I must
Drown in a river
Of tears
So be it
I let you down
You will never know
How sorry I am

FINDING PEACE

Darkness falls
Across the land
The world is quiet
Like there is
No one around
But I feel you
Beside me
I know the secrets
You keep
Locked away inside
You want to know
Why you're fighting
Because you don't
For the life of you
Understand why
Maybe you're fighting
For freedom
For love
For life
For yourself
Stop fighting
Find peace
In your soul

Walk With Me

Walk with me
Hand in heart
We will help each other
Understand
How to go through
There will never
Be a day
That we'll fall apart
So we'll forever be
Together
Hand in heart

A New Relationship

You wanna be
The one to start
A new relationship
Kiss the rain
Run for miles
Just to make
Yourself to where
That person is
You don't wanna go
You don't need to stay
But you know
You must
Get it together
Memories are what
You will grow old with
Make this night
An everlasting memory
Start a new
Relationship

My Blues

Boy, do I
Have the blues
Tears roll down
Like a raging river
I thought you cared
Maybe you do
Maybe you hide it
'Cause your friends are around
Love is not this
This is out of control
You always said I mattered
But no, you lost it
Baby, you lost your mind
Maybe you lost your heart
I don't need this
I want to say goodbye
Saw you with that look in your eyes
I hate to see you
Looking like you're lost and lonely
But you must save your own self
No
I don't need
Your reasons
No more excuses
Please
Begging for it
You can't
Have it anymore

A Friend

I found a new friend
He is a unique friend of mine
He has hidden
Yet a special passion
He accepts me
For who I am
He cares for me
Just like an angel
When I think of him
It rains poetry
The fear in me
It just makes me realize
Just how lucky I am
To have such
A friend

Don't Preach To Me

Don't preach to me
If I have made a mistake
Let me learn from it
In my own way
Don't try to turn around
Everything you've ever
Said to me
Don't disagree
With my decisions
You know
I may actually
Be right on a thing
Or two
I have a mind
Of my own
So don't preach to me
If I have made a mistake
Let me learn from it
In my own way

Remember The Laughter

Remember the laughter
Recall all the tears
Over everything
But nothing at all
You always told me
I could fly
But don't you think
It should be over
Now that you don't know
Who you are
I may never
Remember you
The way we used
To be
The memories have
All disappeared now
Like after the storm
When the sun
Once again
Mysteriously creeps up
On you
Recall the tears
Remember the laughter
Once again

RECYCLE MY HEART

Recycle my heart
You will need it again
Someday
Somehow
Your eyes say no
But your heart
Is saying yes
Though we both know
You've broken it
Recycle my heart
Someday you will need it
Again

You May Find God

Maybe tomorrow
In the afternoon
You know
You may
Find God
Who knows
It is possible
I cry for you
I pray for you
I took the walk
You're walking
Now boy
I've been in your shoes
It is a lonely place
To be
There is not a soul
That you know around
You should
Know yourself
Be your own number one
And with time
Others will love you

The Broken Road

God bless
The broken road
That lead me
Straight to you
I'm alone
When you hold me
I don't feel
The love
I know
I need
So I run away
To find
What I'm missing
In my life
I find myself
Somehow
Again
Missing and endlessly
Needing you
So God bless
The broken road
That lead me
Straight to you

LOVE WILL BE WAITING

Love will be
Waiting at home
She says
Knowing he lied
Once again
Of where
He was going
Wanted to grab him
And tell him
That she knows
Yes, she knows
All about this
Other woman
But instead
She lets him go
Maybe he will be gone
For a few hours
Maybe he will be gone
Forever
Love will be waiting at home
She says
Kowing, he lied
Once again
Of where
He was going

That Fine Saturday

What's up
How is life treating you
Good, I hope
Do you remember
That fine Saturday
Back in the
Good ol' days
When you took my hand
And told me
That you
Were crazy
I laughed, frightened
And asked
What you meant
You smiled
And said
You were crazy
But only for me
That was the first
Time you kissed me
I will never forget
What you said
That fine Saturday

THE RED ROSE

Far off she felt
The red rose at her lips
She wondered who
It could have been from
No letter was left
At the door
Of where the rose
Was found
Motionless people
Of whom it could have been
Rolled through the mind
Of her soul
She had
But no love
That she was aware off
A lonely soul was she
Before even knowing
Who the rose was from
She tenderly cut herself with the thorn
Without even knowing
Slowly fell to the floor
With only blood
On the red rose
She received
At the door
Of where the rose was found

His God

He says he lives
For religion
Though he has
His own motivation
He hears what
He wants
Words mean nothing
Useless conversation
He forgets every word
As soon as you
Leave him
His God
Is different
Than yours
And mine
Sure, he believes
In God
But the way
He believes
Is a mystery
Even to him

How Long I've Loved You

Who knows
How long
I've loved you
Far before
I've loved myself
Love was not
In me
Until I looked
Into your eyes
I should have known
Love was holding my hand
As, with a smile
You introduced yourself
To me
Your blue eyes
Made me lose my thoughts
My hand touched yours
Suddenly
You owned me
My mind
My body
My heart
And my soul
So who knows
How long
I've loved you

My Own Worst Nightmare

I won't leave me alone
I can't get myself
To stay away from me
I don't know
If I hate myself
Maybe love myself
So, please put
Your hands in your pockets
And please
Pull out some hope
For me
It has
Been a
Long day
I don't know me
I am my own
Worst nightmare
My only stranger
I want to know
Who I am
But too afraid
To be disappointed
By whoever that
May be

Is It Cold In Here

Is it cold in here
Or is it just me
Did the room temperature
Just drop
My frozen soul
Is unknown
By you
Happenings are not
On your list
Of things
To do
I don't know you
You don't understand
Did the temperature
Just drop
Is it cold in here
Or is it just you

Lonely Tonight

If I'm gonna be
Lonely tonight
I think
I'd rather be alone
Stay home
Watch movies
Cry myself to sleep
I am used to
Feeling unsafe
And the doors locked
I wonder
What life would be
Like for me
If
If anything
So, if I'm
Gonna be
Lonely tonight
I'd rather
Stay at home
I'd rather
Stay at home tonight

My Eyes Were Tired

My eyes were tired
From crying
I know just how to whisper
And I know just how
To lie
To bare the feeling
Of loneliness
I don't need
To be left alone
In the middle
Of the night
I feel like screaming
But I know
No one will hear me
So what is the point
My eyes are tired
I'm through with crying

It's A Bumpy Ride

Even though
It's a bumpy ride
Keep your head
Above the water
Love will be there
In the end
Keep the faith
You will make it through
Keep on rolling
Is what you must do
It is up to you
If you are
Up to it
I do not live
For someone
Until he lives
For me
I hope you agree
With that
You are a special person
So, keep the faith
Keep believing
In yourself
Even though
It's a bumpy ride

When He Comes Around

When he comes around
He is like an angel
Who holds my heart
In the palm
Of his hands
When he speaks
He moves his lips
With a burning desire
I have lived
On the outside
Of practically everything
One too many times
I have been alone
In the dark
But when I look at him
I realize
That everything
Will be all right
But only if I
Make it that way

Stiff

Stiff as I don't know what
I slowly get up
And bravely stretch
My aching body
I go to the kitchen
Pour myself a cup
Put my regular
Cream and sugar in
And go over
To the window
Slowly sipping
My coffee
I wonder
What the rest
Of the world
Could be up to
My aching body
Slowly eases
As I get dressed
And get ready
For another
Perfectly normal
For me day

It's Hurts To Love You

It hurts
To love you
Because you are
Always loving
In your
Own little world
Thought you loved me
Thought you cared
You don't even know
How to say goodbye
You care
For the impossible
But the impossible
Does not care
For you
I care
For you
But you
Don't care for me
It hurts to love you
So maybe
I should leave you
And start
Painlessly
Loving myself

I Know What Sadness Is

Hi
It's me
Yeah, I know
What sadness is
Loneliness
Has found a home
In me
I do not understand
Why sadness stays
As friends leave
Me crying
And unsure of why
They are all leaving
I don't know
Why he couldn't
Just stay with me
He could not stand
To be near me
I must be untrusty
Because I am afraid
That the truth
Is going to hurt me
How did things
Get so crazy?
Bye
It's me
Yeah, I know
What sadness is

Rhythm Of The Rain

The rhythm
Of the rain
Makes me sleepy
I cry like the angels
For a star
To wish upon
Somewhere
Up there
I know
Someone can hear me
He may not
Be listening
But he can
Surely hear me
When the rain
Finally calms down
So does the rhythm
Of my heartbeat
I fall asleep
Knowing that
Tomorrow will be
A bright
Sunny day

SCARS

We are born innocent
Sometimes
In desperate matters
And shame
We do sinful things
We beg for forgiveness
But we must first
Forgive ourselves
In that way
Our scars from
All our sins
Will be taken away
And to replace
These scars
Will be a mark
Of pure innocence

Tears Of Mourning

Do my tears
Of mourning
Threaten anyone?
I feel like flying
Suddenly
I'm back
Where I started
I feel so confused
I don't know
If I should laugh
Like a barrow
Of monkeys
Or cry
Like a weeping willow
So, I ask
But one final time
Do my tears
Of mourning
Threaten anyone?

Blue Skies

Blue skies are here
Achingly yonder
The flowers
Are weeping
For more
When it rains
And the angel's tears
Gently but firmly
Touch the flowers
It is very
Reassuring
To know
That they
And that everything
Will be all right

CHANGE

Change is good
Seasons change
People change
Feelings change
Sacrifice is good
Memories are endless
I would sacrifice
Tomorrow
Just to
Have you here
Today
Yes, to have
You here today

WEEK DAYS

Except for Monday
Which was never good
Anyway
Tuesday
I've been a
Little sideways
Wednesday
I feel better
Just for spite
Thursday and Friday
Take too long
Before I know it
Saturdays gone
And when Sunday comes
You can bet
That I'm all right

Racism

Racism
Is easy
To define
It is nothing
But a form
Of ignorance
Everyone is a person
With feelings
And a very deep soul
Everybody deserves
And has the right
To be happy
Individuality
Should be a lot
More important
Then pride

LOVE YOURSELF

If one person
Loves you
You have a lot
But if you learn how to
Love yourself
You have it all
Love makes
The world turn
Love makes
The world go 'round
Learning to love yourself
Is the greatest
Love of all

No One Ever Listens

I'm sorry
About the attitude
That you only get
And I only give
When I am with you
But no one else
Will listen to me
My weapon
Are words
My vocabulary
May be a little rusty
But no one else
Has ever listened
To a word
I have ever said
No one has ever
Taken my words to heart
No one has ever
Taken me seriously

Heart Made OF Glass

A heart
Made of glass
So easy to touch
Too easy to break
No one is born
With a broken heart
No
When love and hate collide
They come across
A rough road
To follow
The devil is saying
Go
Take my hand
And go
But the angels
Are crying
Please child
Please stay
So easy to break
A heart
Made of glass

Just Go Ahead

If you want
To call me baby
Just go ahead now
But if you
Would rather
Tell me maybe
Just go ahead now
And if you
Want to buy me flowers
Just go ahead now
But if you
Would rather
Talk for hours
Just go ahead now

SOMEDAY

Someday
I'll have
To disappear
In daylight
And come back
At midnight
And reappear happy

Because I Love You

Passion
I will give you
Fever
Make your temperature rise
Love
You for all that you are
Make you so high
You won't believe
You don't have wings
But boy
I can make you fly
The feeling will be
So incredible
Make your soul
Reach forever
Which continues
For all time
All of this
Because
I love you

The Moment I Treasure

You smile
When you sleep
Every moment with you
Is the moment
I treasure
I stay awake
Watching you
I want to
Wake you up
But I am far
Too scared
To spoil
The precious mood

WITH OR WITHOUT YOU

It is
Tearing up my heart
When I am
With you
But when we are apart
I can feel it too
And no matter
What I do
I feel the pain
With or
Without you

The Picture Kept

Don't call me
The picture kept
Will remind me
My faith
Has faded away
To a far-off place
I gave up looking
The day I lost
My faith in you
Since then
My soul
Has slowly healed
With the help
Of the picture
To remind me

Let God

Let God
Deal with
The things
They do
Because hate
In your heart
Will consume
You too

Pressure, Pain And Broken Promises

Pressure, pain
And broken promises
Is what I am
Going through
'Cause I am
Away from you
Pressure, pain
And broken promises
Is what I am
Going through
And if you have
Never ever, never
Been in love
It is pressure, pain
And broken promises

If You Want My Love

Love is work
And work is hard
Cinderella
Walked upon
Broken glass
Sleeping Beauty
Let a whole
Lifetime pass
Cinderella said to Snow White
"How does love
Get so off course?
All I wanted
Was a white knight
With a good heart
Soft touch
Fast horse
Why is the distance
Between two people
More than they can use?"
Love, hate
The crazy thing
If you want my love
You get
Everything

Lost Hope

Every time
I get my hope lost
I then realize
That what
Could have been
Is much better than
What could never
Be at all

I Am Afraid Of The Thunder

I hear the thunder
Roughly bang against everything
I can see it
With colors of fear
I am afraid of thunder
I do not feel safe at all
Slowly I close my eyes
My thoughts
They fly away
To a place
Where I felt safe before
The sound of the thunder
Is slowing down now
I can still hear raindrops
Oh, but there is that
Sound of thunder again
I am scared
I am not used
To such a frightening sound
I am alone in my room
Too afraid to tell my parents
How scared I am
I wish the thunder would end
I am so afraid of it
The sound the sight
The colors of fear
Make the city so dark
I am afraid
I am afraid
Of the thunder

BRANDI TUCKER

THUNDER AND LIGHTNING

Thunder and lightning
To the naked eye
Are just teardrops from above
But to a soul
With fear of thunder and lightning
It is the end of the world
Trees crashing to make roads unsafe
The sound
Makes your heart pound
The sight
Makes you want
To close your eyes
And never see again
You feel imprisoned
Because you can't move
Your body is shaking
But one step and
You're gone with the wind

I Believe In Yesterday

I believe
In yesterday
It may sound foolish
But the past
Has a huge impact
On my life
On all our lives
These days
People either
Worry about everything
Or nothing at all
I believe
In yesterday

ONE HEARTBEAT AT A TIME

Shhh…
Be quiet
As I hold you
Lay down
Don't wonder
Don't ask any questions
For I have
No answers
Just close your eyes
And relax
Just be
Take it one heartbeat
At a time
Close your eyes
And let your soul unwind
Sooner or later
It will all fall
Into place
We just need to
Take it
One heartbeat
At a time

I Think Of You

Now and then
I think of you
All the things
That we have been through
We walked on water
You and I
Times I thought
That I could fly
Your feelings for me
Felt so real
The love you
Would only reveal
To someone like me
You said you loved me
But now how should
I feel
Happy or sad
Fine with it or sad
Fine with it or mad
Now and then
All the things
That we've been through
Somehow, I always
Think of you

When Children Suffer

I hate it
When children suffer
Being blamed
For something
That they had
Nothing to do with
It doesn't seem fair
They cry
For good reason
But for nothing at all
Jealous comes
Too easily
They see someone
With two parents
A father who
Gets along with
The mother
But children
See clearer
Than we do
So listen to your children
Talk to them
Ask questions
Be a friend
I hate it
When children suffer

I Found Love

I found love
It is beauty
I see color
At last
The world
Is no longer
Black and white
Blue sky's
White sand
Beauty is
Anywhere you find it
It can be in a song
In a heartbeat
In who you are
I found love
It is beauty
I found love
In me

It Isn't Easy

It doesn't seem
Like much anymore
No
It isn't easy
The will to be strong
Is weak
By reality
I wish
The real world
Would just stop
Hassling me
And you
And the world
It just doesn't seem
Like much anymore

A Broken Home

A broken home
She picks up the pieces
Of broken glass
And a broken heart
They send her
Broken arrows
They expect her
Just to understand
She spends
Half her life
On bended knee
Begging somebody to change
And the other half
Praying to God
That they never would
It only gets her
Twice as lost
And it all
Turns out the same
But all that begging
Finally does
Somebody good
In another broken home

I Have Sinned

I have sinned
He cried
Looking for the wings
Of an angel
He was afraid
He wasn't going
To make it
To heaven
He prayed
Fell asleep
And fell into
An angels arms
I have sinned
He cried

TIME

Time
Is like a river
It slows down
And passes you by
It goes so fast
When you're having fun
But slows down
'Cause you're alone
Time
Is like a river
It slows down
And passes you by

All I Need

All I need
Is a miracle
A young
Strong
Clueless man
To memorize
Each thing I say
Someone who
Will think
I am worth
Sticking it out for
Someone to surround
And shower me
With the love
That I long for
A heart
That is young
A man with a mind
A body with a soul
And a heart full of love

Mama

Mama
I found someone
Just like you said
Would come along
Although
He may not be
A rich tycoon
He is still the one
I think that I
Shall marry
And maybe
Have a kid
Or two
I know you think
I'm nuts right now
But I think
You are too
Mama he's lazy
Lazier than me
He never does
The housework
He leaves it all to me
I never hated dust
'Till it got
The worst of me
Mama he's lazy
He's lazier than me

ALL YOU ARE

All you are
Is all I want
I care for you
Because you're you
You are not demanding
But you
Do demand respect
All you are
Is all I want

How You Loved Me

I am back
To what I knew
Before you
I remember
How you loved me
Every single breathe
You took
Was mine
I remember
How you loved me
Time was all we had
'Till the day
We said good bye
Please
Don't run away
On what we have
Together
Apart
It is nothing
I am back
To what I knew
Before you

Anything For You

I'd do
Anything
For you
But give you up
You hurt me
Through and through
But you know
I am strong
I'm strong enough
To say I tried
But far too weak
To say goodbye
No
You'll never
Hear me crying
But inside I
Feel like dying
I'd do
Anything for you

I'll Be

I'll be captivated
I'll hang from your lips
And I'll be
Your crying shoulder
I'll be
No reason
For suicide
And I'll be
Better when
I'm older
I'll be
The greatest
Friend of you life

BEING PERFECT

All my life
I try to be perfect
Knowing it's impossible
I still try
Being perfect is
Something no one
Has ever been perfect at
I want to
Know how it feels
To matter
To make a difference
All my life
I try to be perfect

A Thousand Needles

A thousand needles
Pierce my heart
As you look away
With sadness
In your eyes
Is there a chance
Am I worth it
You tell me as
A thousand needles
Pierce my heart

BRANDI TUCKER

Think Of Me

Think of me
As you kiss
Her lips
I bet
You never
Go out
And kiss the rain
With her
Like you and I did
So please
Think of me
As you kiss
Her lips

I Try Not To Laugh

I try not to laugh
But I think
You're funny
When you're mad
I'm the kind of gal
Who laughs
At a funeral
Don't understand me yet?
Well you soon will
I'm silly
Plus bonkers
As well as nuts
I try not to laugh
But I think
You're funny
When you're mad

Never Forget

I will never forget
The anger
In his eyes
When I
Disagreed with his plan
He slowly
Walked away
And left me
With a handful
Of dust
I can't believe
For the life of me
That boy has
A heart of stone
No
I'm sure
His tears fall
When he feels
All alone
In his eyes
I will
Never forget

Throw Away The Past

Throw away the past
My child
Nothing lasts forever
Yesterday is
Just a memory
Tomorrow is
A scary event about to be
Understand
That life is
Not perfect
Nor is the world
Or people
My child
Throw away the past

Steal My Breath

Steal my breath
As your beauty
Is my love
And my living proof
And survival
Tell them
To leave you alone
You are
My crying shoulder
You feel my pain
You cry before I do
Over fear in my soul
I love you
Steal my breath
As your beauty
Is my love
I love you

Make Up Your Mind

Make up your mind
Decide on
One or the other
This, that
Them, us
Him, her
What kind of man are you?
You must be scared
I cannot afford
One more tear
Nor can you
So please
Make up
Your mind

It's About Forgiveness

I've been trying
To get down
To the heart
Of the matter
But my will
Gets weak
From the distance
Of our bodies
And I think
It's about
Forgiveness
Forgiveness
Even if
You don't love me
Anymore

Heart On The Mend

This is the last
Worthless evening
That you'll ever spend
Just give me
A chance to prove
Your heart is on the mend
This the last
Worthless evening
That you'll have to spend
'Cause it won't be long
'Till your poor
Little heart
Is on
Is on the mend

Seventeen

There was a guy
Setting my dreams
On fire
Back in the class
I was sinking
So fast
Drowning in
My own desire
You can
Love somebody
That is a natural fact
But the hard part
Is finding somebody
To love you back
You can love somebody
The way you only
Dream of being loved
But you must
Love yourself

The Pain

The only thing
That has ever been
Just for me
Was the pain
They don't know it
Never do they feel it
They just stair
At darkened eyes
With a river
Of endless tears
After the way
They treat me
They lie to me
And cheat me
They know
They're driving
Me mad
I give up
I quit
No, this time it's over
I can no longer
Live my life knowing
That the only thing
That has ever been
Just for me
Was the pain

There Are No Secrets

There are no secrets
No angels at my door
When you look at me
Or call my name
Or touch my hand
I fall from the clouds
In heaven
Into your arms

EYEING AN ANGEL

She seems sad
He could tell
Eyeing an angel
With sorrow
Crossing her lips
Her eyes are weeping
Though no tears arouse her
Bare lips
With the scent
Of heavenly angels
Green eyes
That he could only breathe
The shape of her breasts
Showed a firm soul
But a weakened heart
Her blonde hair
Long as a river
Rushing across the shore
A tempered mind
Full of thoughts
She could not control or
Make disappear
The essence
Of her lips
Made him lose his breath
She seems sad
He could tell
Eyeing an angel
With sorrow
Crossing her lips

BRANDI TUCKER

Finding Faith

Out of faith
She lies cold
And ashamed
But in a memory
He is calling
Her again
Gently feeling guilty
Opens her eyes
To only a bare soul
Empty and used
Praying for what she needs
Whatever that may be
Looks in the mirror
Stares at empty eyes
No feeling in her eyes
She splashes her tanned face
With cool water
Takes a second look
Her eyes change color
Mystically she feels
Better again
Finding faith
Was easier
Than she thought possible

SEEING HER BEAUTY

A Blind man
Could see her beauty
Though with perfect vision
She can't
Crying for mercy
Her soul has just
Graduated from heartache
Thrown on the cruel streets
She makes the best
By being someone's angel
Though with perfect vision
She can't
A blind man
Could see her beauty

Chill

When it feels like
The world is
On your shoulders
And all the madness
Has got you going crazy
Take a breather
Empty your mind
Refill your soul with magic
And the rhythm
You can't live without
Come on join the fun
Have a good time
Before long you will
Forget about the worries
On your mind
Celebrate
Hear the music
Just plain and simply
Chill

Don't Send Me Away

Those moon lights
Steal my soul
And light my hunger
Those moon light desires
Haunt me
Do you want me?
Do I want you
To want me?
The hunger within me
Is wild
Don't send me
Don't send me away

Under The Stars

They made love
Under the stars
Falling for
Their every wish
He held her tight
She felt safe
He has been
Running scared
Till he found her
She was in the wrong place
At the right time
Then they found
Themselves
And each other
Making love
Under the stars
Falling for
Their every wish

A Miracle

Amen
She said
Praying for
A miracle
To bring
Her soul at ease
Calm winds
Stopped the thunder
The power
In the house
And in her soul
Came on again
Amen
She said
Thankful for
A miracle

The Abuse

She held
A sharp knife
In her hand
Dwelling on
The past
When she was stabbed
Abused by
The memory
No matter
How much therapy
She had
The abuse
Would never end
She put
The sharp knife
Back in the cupboard
Closed her eyes
And cried
Forget the abuse
Nor would
She let it
Happen again

Never Make Sense

Some things
In life
Will never
Make sense
Like who
Or what
Maybe where
Possibly when
Always ask why
I wonder how
Some things
In life
Just never
Make sense

What Is It Like In Heaven

What is it like
In heaven?
Does everyone
Have a rainbow
To ride on?
Or do you make angels
Go down to earth
To help a lost soul?
Do you
Play endless games
On Heavenly clouds?
Or do you
Live in a
Perfect world?
What is it like
In Heaven?

COLORS

Red
Is the rose to your lips
Green
Is the grass
That you lay on
Blue
Is the sky
In the hot afternoon
Gray
Is the cool
Night light above you
White
Is the cloud your lips
Softly blow away
Yellow
Is the hot sun that strips
Away the sadness in
Your eyes
Red
Is the rose to your lips

If My Best Isn't Good Enough

If my best
Isn't good enough
Then how can
It be
Good enough for two?
I can't work
Any harder
Than I do
My soul is broken
My head is pounding
My heart is telling fairy tales
My dear
If my best
Isn't good enough
Than how can
It be
Good enough for two?

Hold On

Hold on
To everything
You believe in
If it matters to you
That is all
That must matter
Smile
Enjoy life
Hold on
To anything
You believe in

One, Two I miss you

One, two
I miss you
Three four
I need more
Five six
I would not miss
spending one
More night
With you
Seven eight
Be my date
Nine ten
Let's kiss again
Ten nine
Boy you're fine
Eight seven
Take me to heaven
Six five
At last
I am alive
Four three
Make love to me
Two one
Let's have some fun
Boy I love you

Like A Runaway Train

My heart
Is pounding
In my chest
Like a runaway train
When will I be
Rescued by
The arms
Of love?
More like
Will it ever happen?
I am always alone
Even with a crowd
Of strangers
I have known
All my life
My mind
Is full of endless thoughts
And never answered questions
My heart
Is pounding
In my chest
Like a runaway train

Don't Close Your Eyes

Don't close your eyes
Everyone falls
Why don't you get up?
What if the world
Was a little
More perfect?
Would you stop caring?
Would you take the leap?
What if the world
Were a little more perfect?
Would you live again?
Maybe just for me?
What am I to do?
Would you take the leap?
Would you open your eyes?
Maybe if you had a diamond
In your eyes
Where is the sorrow that you see
When no one else
Can hear your dreams?
So, whatever you do
Don't close your eyes

Emeralds And Mountains

Emeralds and mountains
Color you
Wonderful
Sorry
I couldn't
Help but stare
And you're
My survival
You're my
Living proof
That diamonds
Are beauty
When they're bare

Zero To Sixty

My heart was going
Zero to sixty
As his eyes
Glared to my direction
My mind was suddenly blank
Like a piece of paper
You have several thoughts
But you are not sure
Which one to write
My lips wanted,
So bad to make their way
To where he was
I hoped his lips
Were juicy and salty
As my lips curled into my mouth
The darkness
Made it easy
To turn his head
As he did, our eyes met
Our hearts were going
Zero to sixty

Waiting For A Call

I sit in the kitchen
Waiting for a call
I know in my heart
I will never get
I treated him like a fool
But still, I will love him
For the rest of my life
I pray,
Begging for a miracle
The oven beeps
I pick up the phone
I must be silly
I gather my thoughts together
Eat like I'm not nervous
I sit in the kitchen
Waiting for a call
I know in my heart
I will never get

It's Been One Week

It's been
One week
Since you looked at me
Drop your eyes
And I can see
You're angry
Five days
Since I tackled you
You just did
What I thought
You were gonna do
Three days
In the living room
You know
It wasn't my fault
So, what are
We to do?
Yesterday
You just smiled at me
And it will
Still be
Two days
Till I say
I'm sorry

Flying Backwards

Flying backwards
On a pair
Of dangerous wings
Never aware of
Where to go
You carry
Everybody's smile
On your lips
You're an eagle
Silver eyes
Make it easy
To preach
To a long
Lost friend
Going crazy
Flying north
Of nowhere
South of somewhere
Without direction
Life is nothing
So, you are
Flying backwards
On a pair
Of dangerous wings

Love Me Too

I'm so much
In love with you
But your friends
Have got you thinking
And it's affecting you
I don't know what to do
'Cause I'm so
In love with you
It doesn't matter
What your friends do
They're just jealous
Of me and you
I know
That this feeling
I'm feeling
Just won't let me go
I know it makes me happy
To be in love with you
No one loves you
Like I love you
I still love you
So please
Oh please
Love me too

I'm Lonely

I'm lonely
She cried
Wishing her father
Could hear her
He takes her out
But they do nothing at all
Tears
He will never see
She loves her father
More than anything
But she can't tell him
How she feels in her heart
I'm lonely
She cried
Wishing her father
Could hear her

BRANDI TUCKER

She Found Someone

She found someone
Yay
She met him
At a church sale
She helped him pick out
Some clothes
He is beautiful
She promised him
They would be together again
He has a beautified body
He is tall
Eighteen years of age
Smart
Sassy
Sexy
Yay
She found someone

Before You Play The Game

I'll take a breath
And clear your sweet head
I dreamt
Another girl was in bed
With you
You just laughed
And denied the proof
Fine
Least 'till
I think about it
I'm not so dumb
Boy, you better listen
Cut it out
Listen to all the rules
Before you play the game
So, don't say
You love me
I really don't
Think that's fair

Do Drop Inn

Do drop in
At the
Do drop inn
At the do drop inn
My friend
If you
Don't drop in
At the
Do drop inn
I'll kick you
In the chin
So, do drop in

Let's Talk

Now
Let's talk
I will
Pour you a cup
Of coffee
Need an ear to bend?
So be it
My ears are bendable
Come on
Talk to me
Let me be
Your crying shoulders
Let me be
The greatest
Friend of your life
Now
Let's talk

I Tune In

I tune in
I turn it on
Remember each thing
That you said
Crying on my knees
Begging for your shoulder
To cry on
My eyes are wet
My mouth is dry
Either take me in
Or let me be
Far from glamour
Your heart is returned
To that rainy night
We were locked out
We danced to the sound
Of the thunder
You laughed
When you saw
God's tears
Fall from my eyes
I remember
Everything about you
I tune in
I turn it on
Remember each thing
That you said

WISHING REAL DREAMS

With a glowing heart
I see thee rise
As I look
Out my window
Naked eyes
Look in the mirror
Searching for
Perfectly visible beauty
A blind person
Could see
Blinded
By the beauty
I see
My mind disappear
To a place
Where he is holding me
Uncontrollably whispering
Soft secrets
We both share
Wishing real dreams
Were reality
Sip my coffee
So my tongue doesn't burn
Stare at an angel
Who doesn't know
He is one

Would You Trust Me

Would you trust me
If I promised
I would never lie
As your eyes wander
Carefully seeking for a perfectly
Visible answer
Questions in your mind
You write them down
Meaning to send them to me
But your hope
Is not that strong
You burn them
Each with a silent prayer
I can hear you
It's so amazing
How your voice
Breaks through
If I promised
I would never lie
Would you trust me

Now I lay Me

Now I lay me
Down to sleep
I hope and pray
You're in my dreams
My eyes gently close
As my mind sees you
Walking on the desert sand
Hot, but cool
Your eyes are heated
With the love I gave you
When I was with you today
So, now I lay me
Down to sleep
I hope and pray
You're in my dreams

THE SILENCE

The silence
Is everything
I need to hear
I look in your eyes
For reassurance
That everything
Will be alright
I see your eyes
As a river
I've been
Saved from
Rescued by the arms
Of love
The silence
Is everything
I need to hear

I Feel Blue Today

I feel blue today
So I put
My blue jeans on
You know
The skintight pair
I put on
My blue silk blouse
Put my makeup on
In the same order
As I always do
I first put my
Powder on
My blush
The eye makeup
Then finally
My rose lipstick
I no longer
Feel blue today

As Tears Rose

As tears rose
To her lips
She tasted
The sweetness
And cruelty
Of his being
Her long thick nails
Softly squeezed his lips
Wishing she could
Only tell him
Or say, even what he did to her
The night before
But only fools rush in
She told herself
Believing every small detail
Enlarging the company
Of his tough lips
Memoryless
He gave her
A clueless look
Seeking for answers
She'd refuse to reveal
Dried her tears
With a salty tasting kiss
She again
Loved him for
Who he was
Who he is
Who he ever wished to be
As tears once again
Rose to her lips

CAN'T FALL ASLEEP

Middle of the night
I can't fall asleep
Shadows on the walls
Are so obsolete
I just stay awake
With endless thoughts
Running around my brain
I never should
Have run away
From nothing I made such
A big deal about
My mind was relying
On a fairy tale
My heart
Was more unsure
Than I can ever say
I find it hard to sleep
These nights
I don't know what my problem is
But I know for a fact
I don't need medication
Middle of the night
I can't fall asleep

BRANDI TUCKER

ALL THAT I HAVE

Why do I give you
All that I have
When you leave me
With nothing
My heart is broken
From your nonsense
You must
Take over
Take on more responsibility
It's all in you
Up to you
What you do with it
Leave me with pieces
Of a broken heart
Or stay
And lift my spirits
Why do I give you
All that I have
When you leave me
With nothing

I Love You

I love you
But sorry
Doesn't cut it
I'm tired of your foolishness
Running away
From what is real
Making relationships fake
Your eyes speak your mind
My lips speak my heart
You fly away
When you need somebody
But then it's too late
To go back to what you needed
You shouldn't doubt me
You should respect
Who you are
Now you know
That with all my mind
Body
Heart and soul
I love you
But sorry
Doesn't cut it
I love you

Carry on

Carry on smiling
And the world
Will smile with you
About the past
Time is precious
Life is a box
Of chocolates
You never know
What you will get
No time soon
Will the world stop
'Cause you're sad
Carry on smiling
And the world
Will smile with you

When I Say I Lied

Believe me
When I say
I lied
I want to be
Just friends
Yeah right
Look at you
You're just too hot
To handle
Letting go of you
Would be a
Hugh mistake
So honey
Believe me
When I say
I lied
I want to be
More than just friends

THE BREAK OF DAWN

Tonight
We'll fight
The break
Of dawn
Come tomorrow
Tomorrow I'll be gone
So many words
I could say
But no reflection
Of the past
Is necessary now
I must say goodbye now
Tonight
We'll fight
The break of dawn

I Love You More Than Myself

I smile
And take both
Of your hands
In mine
And try to explain
Sometimes when you're so sad
For so long
You can't see the beauty
Right in front of you
Sometimes the pain
Is so strong
It swallows your good sense
And there you are
Laying on the floor
Nothing moving
Not even a single heartbeat
There you are dead
Leaving everything
And everyone you love, behind
The sadness
Has just taken over your life
I love you
More than myself
Goodbye

LIFE

Life is pigs and tails
Getting dirty
And brushing off
All the hatred
You felt yesterday
Love is a rose and pain
Beauty and the pain you feel
By loving one who wants you so much
He forgets to love you

I'VE BEEN WANTED

I've been wanted
By someone so much
He forgot to love me
Then loved by one
Who forgot to want me
Lesson well learned
I then began to learn
To want to love myself
If he wants me
I must get enough self-control
And self-abuse
To gain his trust
In me
I must want to love
Then love to want myself

Paying For Your Mistakes

Paying for your mistakes
Because you're gone
Questions
I lip to a stranger
But no sound comes out
This can't be
What will go on
For the rest of my life
I'm young
Please, I need, no, deserve
A chance to live
And be sheltered
By angels
Who will keep my memory
Away from me
Because you're gone
I'm paying
For your mistakes

The Pleasure I Have

The pleasure I have
Of being with you
Is so pure
It's the softness
Of a rose bud
But the sharpness
Of the thorn
I need to hear
The softness
Of your whisper
And the roughness
Of your scream
To fall into you
And dream
Of a perfect world
Where only two people
Can appreciate the pleasure I have
Of being with you

MALE BONDING

Male bonding
Interesting concept
Burping at on another
Giving each other noogies
Having uncontrollable weggies
What's a girl to do?
Grin and bare it?
Dump him as though he has
A problem or split personality?
Get him therapy?
Male bonding
Interesting concept

Being An Individual

Isn't being an individual
More important
Then being the same as everyone?
I think it is
People learn by listening
But by hearing
You walk the footsteps
Of a stranger
And learn things
You didn't know you never knew
So, isn't being an individual
More important
Then being the same as everyone?

Over My Head

Over my head
You talk about life
In a sense
I don't understand
No poetry
No figure of speech
You talk
'Cause you don't know
How to feel
Reality is not basic
You ask questions
'Cause it's all over
Over your head
Under your feet
The location of who you are
Is everywhere
But nowhere to be found
Like air
You're invisible
But everybody needs you
Once again
Over my head

A Phantasm Of You

Just last night
I had a phantasm of you
An illusion or vision
'Cause you're an absent person
I see you every day
At the restaurant
I ask how you are doing
The more I ask
The worse it gets
The more it seems
We're falling apart
Begging for your eyes
To clash with mine
I see sadness
It is so real
I can't pretend
Who you are
A stranger I knew forever
Just last night
I had a phantasm of you

Your Passion

Your passion
And your beauty
Has saved me from my sins
I see what beauty is
Naughty words
Cross your lips
As I walk away
Saying a prayer
Folding my hands
Closing my eyes
Obviously, I'm praying
I whisper what I feel
And you know it
You know my every word
Your passion
And your beauty
Has saved me once again

Youth

Youth goes hand and hand
With foolish pride
A teardrop falls
As you feel
Like you're
About to die
Nothing you can do
You feel hopeless
And unloved
You have nothing
Nothing to live for
Or to believe in
Loneliness has taken
Happiness away
It feels
Like it's been years
Since you smiled
Suicide feels like
The greatest
Friend of your life
No one holds you
Just for the love of it
No love exists anymore
You don't have
A crying shoulder
Youth goes hand and hand
Someone does love you
Someone holds your hand
A crying shoulder
Is all you need
Now that you have it
You can live
But live forever

BRANDI TUCKER

I Used To Call You Friend

I used to
Call you friend
I guess time
Wasn't that kind
You decided who you were
I am so confused now
Never am I aware
Of what to expect
Will you cry
When something funny happens
Will you laugh at me
When I feel like
My world is about to end
I don't know you anymore
You changed who you were
My heart is sad
Do you know
What I think about
Late at night
When I can't sleep
I think of how life used to be
When we'd laugh
Until we cried
Then laughed because we cried
I now wonder
Do you remember
When I used to
Call you friend
Now I look at you
And I realize
I used to call you friend
I guess time just wasn't that kind

There Is A Life

Little child
Don't you know
That there's a life
And it's gonna
Shine right through
Your eyes
Get higher
Go under
Stay crazy
What do you think
Life is like
Why do you
Waste your time
On the past
Is it because
You can't tell the future
Little child
I promise
There is a life

Untied For Once

Build up your confidence
So you can be
Untied for once
Wake up
Who cares about
Those who only
Talk too much
Don't live your life
Being anybody's fool
When it's through
Hey it's through
You shouldn't
Hang off trees
Trying to impress someone
Be who you are
And proud of it
Let God deal
With the things they do
'Cause hate in your heart
Will consume you too
Don't be absent
From where you wish to be
Hang on honey child
A broken heart can't be that bad
So please
Build up your confidence
So you can be
Untied for once

Shy Away

Shy away
Don't come again
I don't need to see
Your bleeding eyes
Begging for mercy
Closing your eyes
To hide shy tears
I never will forget
How you look
But I never will remember
What you are wearing
With wet eyes
And dry lips
Your heart is frozen
'Cause you're not
Being open
And honest with me
Or yourself
I don't wish to see
Your bleeding eyes
So shy away
Don't come again

WHEN YOU CLOSE YOUR EYES

Can you hear me
When you close your eyes
Can you see only with your soul
Were you blinded
By the light you couldn't live without
Do you breathe
Every word I said
When we talked
On the telephone
One moment with you
Is an everlasting memory
One moment without you
Is forever
When you close your eyes
Can you hear me

TRUE ME TO THE LIES

True me
To the lies
You will be buried with he cries
Can he spread his wings
Like angels
Can he break
Out of the grind
When will we ever learn
He learned as a child
To never tell a lie
He's talking to his angel
Who has a stronger power
Then he could ever wish for
He takes his weapons
And throws them out the window
He has been a soldier
Heaven knows he is no saint
So, he whispers
True me to the lies
I will only
Be buried with

What Matters Is Your Heart

Who will be loving you next
Some old fool
Who's writing bad cheques
Sometimes I wonder
If I'll ever
See you again
If not
I guess
I will always have
The memories
But please
Do not ever leave your dreams
Locked up inside
What matters is your heart
Forget about the notion
My blood runs
As red as yours
Don't give up
I will always
Sing and write about you
So don't wish for
What you don't have
Be thankful for what
You do have now
And please remember
That what matters
Is your heart

It Took A Million Years

It took a million years
Of progress handed down
On silver wings
Something cute about
Burning out
Is better than fading away
As sure as the sunset burns
I stay awake
Thinking of long-lost time
And I wonder
When will we ever learn
The lesson is in front of us
But we look far beyond that
And Charlie
Lays there laughing
And he's laughing in his grave
He will die tomorrow half a man
It took a million years
Of progress handed down
On silver wings
But we are now known
As angels this time

The Greatest Teacher

The greatest teacher
I've ever had
Her name is Annie Wilkenson
She was my
Grade two teacher
She was born, I believe
In England
She taught me more than just math
And what a child
Usually learns
At such a young age
She taught me
How to love
And love who
I would ever be
Well, Annie
Look at me now
Thanks for the Christmas story
In the hospital
I still have and will be buried with
The tape you made for me
I will always remember
Never forget
The greatest teacher
I've ever had
Her name is Annie Wilkenson

Cleveland Park

Cleveland Park
I've never had the pleasure
To go and visit
But I have heard
Nice things about the place
The beaches are hot
The nights are cool
The people are pleasant
What more
Could you ask for
Cleveland Park
I just may find
The pleasure to go and visit

The Rhythm Of Life

The rhythm of life
Soft and loud whispers
You hear unknown angels
Sing to whoever has the heart
To listen
They sing about anything
To keep you by their side
And that my friend
Is the rhythm of life

Thundering Night

How strange
Is a thundering night
Nothing turned on
But the fire
Frozen hands
Touch the stars
Eagerly waiting
For any wish
Never are we aware
Of whom we hurt before the rain
But swear we will never
Hurt again
How strange is the thundering night

SOMEBODY SPECIAL

She is going to be somebody
He spoke
Watching his little girl
Lay helpless
Under the blanket
Gently kissed
Her tiny fingers
He knows
She would be special
Twenty years later
Now a woman
She is still a little girl
Daddy gently touches
Her tiny hand
And whispers
I knew you were special
And I knew
You would be somebody

Not Living In Black And White

I realized something today
I am not living
In black and white
Took me long enough
To realize it
Blue ocean
Grey skies
Golden stars
Green grass
Red roses
I realized I am not
Living in
Black and white

What You Are Is Beautiful

What you feel
Is what you are
And what you are
Is beautiful
I'm not talking
About physical looks
Though you are cute
I'm talking
More along the lines of
Your mind, body
Heart and soul
You care about others
You have a deep soul
And incredible eyes
What you feel
Is what you are
And baby
What you are
Is beautiful

The Rhythm Of The Night

My heart is full
My mind is empty
I fall asleep
To the rhythm
Of the night
At last, there I am
Swept away
By my prince
In a fairy tale
Only is reality
An unrealistic part of me
But only in my dreams
I see the sky open up
And I wonder if
It wants to take me away
To a perfect and
Beautiful place
My dreams
Are my own
No one can take them
Away from me
A dream
Is the greatest
Friend of my life
Good always wins
Disbelievers loose
I fall asleep
To the rhythm of the night

The Sweetness Of Her Perfume

He smells the sweetness
Of her perfume
Dry roses of a poisoned soul
Crossed his mind
The world is full
Of beautiful scents
But he will never
Have the pleasure
Of the same essence again
Scarred lips
He doesn't have the strength
To kiss her hand
Clueless of their conversation
He ends up
Wild eyed and crazed
Knowing tomorrow
May not be kind
He seeks for answers
In her soft blue eyes
Sees the meaning of life
Without thinking
Kisses her flavorful
Yet bare mouth
And again, he smells
The sweetness of her perfume

WHEN YOU SMILE

You're beautiful
When you smile
I may not
See it very often
But when I do
You are like
A rose
on a summer morning
Just fed by the rain
How strange
It may seem
To be you
But you know
I only wish
You knew that
You are beautiful
When you smile

I'm Lonely Daddy

Daddy I'm lonely
She cried to the wind
Knowing that if he
Dare to hear her
It would be a sin
Lying to the
Wild wind
She tells herself
She is all right
And that
She's only
Going through
A rough phase
Her father
Still thinks of her
As a little girl
Free from fear
Free of any problems
I'm lonely Daddy
She cried
Knowing it would
Be a sin
If he dares
To hear her

Like The Wind

Unlike the sun
I see darkness
Unlike the moon
I only see light
Unlike the stars
Shining over my shoulders
And the trees
Magically being moved
Surely dancing
By the invisible wind
You can't see it
But you know
It's there
Like an ache
Deep in your heart
That feeling
One moment it's there
Then it disappears
Like the wind

BRANDI TUCKER

Open Arms

Open arms
But never for me
Lonely tears
I cry alone
I find it hard
To hold on
I want to scream
But I know
In my heart
And my soul
That no one
Will hear me
I walk alone
I feel empty
I have a hole
In my heart
And it is
So wide
I feel
Like I am
Sinking deeper
Every day
I walk alone
With open arms

For You I Will

I will cross the ocean for you
I will go and give you the moon
I will be your hero
Your strength
Anything you need
I will be your sun in the sky
I won't make
You wait for all time
I promise you
For you, I will
These arms will
Be your shelter
These arms
Won't let you down
I love you so much
I would do anything for you
For you
I will lay my heart on the line
Baby, for you
I live and would die
I promise you
For you, I will

What Does My Future Hold

What does my future hold
Is it love
Could it be
The career of my dreams
Will I be
Hot, rich and famous
Oh
I wonder
What does
My future hold

GOOD NIGHT

Eleven o'clock
Almost midnight
Time to curl up
In my bed
Thinking of practically
Everything
Moments later
My mind is a blank
I pray and wish
For, but another day
Though I don't know
What it holds
I want to live for only tomorrow
One precious day
At a time
Again, it is
Almost midnight
Good night

Index

www.ingramcontent.com/pod-product-compliance
Lightning Source LLC
Chambersburg PA
CBHW060239050426
42448CB00009B/1521